The Power of Conscious Dying

JOY TIANYUN WU, Ph.D., DAOM, L.Ac.

Conscious living is
the true happiness of
life !

Tianyun Wu
吴天云 09-07-2018

ISBN-13: 978-1-7323538-8-6

HJI PRESS

885-A Olive Avenue
Novato, CA 94945
Regarding this book, please visit
www.heavenlyjoyinstitute.org
Cover art by Dunja Kacic-Alesic and Aurora
Robathan-Wu

DEDICATION

I dedicate this book to my
wonderful parents.
Both are storytellers of
Taoist traditional cultures.

ii

iii

CONTENTS

CHAPTER 13

ADVANTAGES OF NATURAL
CONSCIOUS DYING (NCD)

GLOSSARY

REFERENCES

ABOUT THE AUTHOR

ACKNOWLEDGMENTS

I would like to express my deep gratitude to my friends, patients, and students who gave me the chance to observe the dying and death process itself, and who put their trust in my hands to help their loved ones. Gratitude to my mother who has passed on so many wonderful stories, and to all who made this book possible.

I want to express my appreciation to all my friends and colleagues who have helped me expand my consciousness and knowledge about dying and death, and who assisted my work involving in the project of natural conscious dying. I also want to express my appreciation to my friends who have helped me in reading, proofreading, editing, and making this book better.

People I would like to thank are: Billy Moran, Gigi Ho Ph.D., Rayde Staton, Xiurong Ma, Ruth Angela, Vinh Tran, Victoria Malco Ph.D., Lobsang Tsering, Guihua Wang, BinBin Beecher, Veronica Laboure-

Slaughter, Jenny Francisco, Ruth Angela, Dana Lomax, Theresa Vetorilo, Donna Call DAOM, L.Ac., Laura Sheehan R.N., D.C., William Robathan, Leanne Thorne, Sharon Voytac, Mondi Safa, Cloudia Charters, and Sandi Rizzo.

I have special gratitude to these last four people; Kim Scudder R.N., Debra Gorman DAOM, L.Ac., Susan Zipp, and Heather Thompson Ph.D. who helped me refine details and logic for the last stage of writing and editing. And, special thanks to Mario Andreis and Zihong Gorman for book proofreading, formatting, and printing.

Also, special thanks to two talented artists who helped illustrate the image for this book's cover. One is my 14-year-old daughter, Aurora Robathan-Wu, who created the conceptual illustration for the cover. Aurora has a keen eye for color and is able to bring the concept of conscious dying into a drawing. Dunja Kacic-Alesic is a talented fine-arts creative illustrator, and often brings me surprises with her refined illustrations. Their efforts made a vivid illustration about the process of a body to soul transition.

Finally, I'm deeply grateful to my family, my sisters, and parents for their continuing support and unconditional love, traditions, and wisdom.

AUTHOR'S FOREWORD

As a healer I have a passion to help all people live and die well.

Before I became a Traditional Chinese Medicine (TCM) doctor, I worked for 20 years in the area of modern life sciences as a research scientist. In the early years after college I was a microbiologist and came to US for a master's degree program in Plant Pathology at Ohio State University, Columbus, Ohio. Later, I continued in a doctoral program in molecular biology and received my Ph.D. degree in 1998.

My first postdoctoral research scientist position was at the University of California, San Francisco. It was a booming time for modern molecular biology, biotechnology, and drug discovery. In the San Francisco Bay Area, I worked nearly ten years as a cellular and molecular biologist. I was also involved in a great amount of research related to biochemistry. I held the position of a bench scientist, handing on many new technologies and methods for DNA cloning, isolation, and purification, sequencing, protein expression, and so on. Most of this work extended into cancer cell research. In concert with this, I spent a couple of years investigating DNA markers of cancer cells.

My very last research project was in the area of using human embryonic stem cells in neuron regeneration. During the last three months of this project I often heard a voice saying, "Using stem cells as medicine is going to be too expensive, not many people can benefit from it." One morning on the way to my lab, while climbing up the stairs, a voice came into my head again asking, "Are you going to do this for the rest of your life?" I was shocked. I replied to that voice in my mind that I had been involved in academic research throughout my whole life, I didn't have any idea about any other thing I could do except engage in research in life science.

In retrospect, it was an awakening of my inner self. My job ended a few weeks after hearing 'that voice' and it set a milestone for my career change. About one month later I experienced an acupuncture treatment and it brought me a great and deeply insightful understanding of the human condition and its medicine. This made me switch my understanding of a healthy human life from this cellular aspect of DNA and biochemistry changes to a cosmic connection of the human body as a whole, cohesive entity.

I found Acupuncture and Traditional Chinese Medicine far more simple, natural, and effective. This ancient life science offers a much deeper and wider knowledge about the existence of the human being in the universe and gives an insight into many diseases that we could never figure out from petri-dishes or DNA sequences alone. Even today, I am still fascinated and deeply appreciative of this ancient wisdom about life that has a myriad of dimensional connections to the universe and the individual self.

It has been more than ten years at this time of writing since this career change. During this time, I received a master's degree and became a licensed acupuncturist in the state of California, later received a Doctoral degree in Acupuncture and Oriental Medicine (DAOM). Over the past eight years, I have served as a professor in the masters and doctoral programs of acupuncture and traditional Chinese medicine at the University of Eastern and Western Medicine, Sunnyvale, California. I also own and operate a Chinese medicine and acupuncture clinic, located in Novato, California.

My positions as professor and clinical doctor complement each other and both have strengthened my passion for Traditional Chinese Medicine. This experience has also deepened my understanding of human medicine and has specifically helped me understand that all levels of healing and care, not only the physical level, contribute equally to our well-being. There is so much that doctors will miss if they fail to regard a human being as a whole person replete with emotions and spirituality. Ancient traditional medicines are both practical and intangible treasures which invite humans to see each other as whole beings, without the separation into mind, body, and spirit.

In my practice, I treat people across the complete spectrum of life, from birth to death. Mostly I encourage them to live harmoniously with nature so that they can be free from chronic diseases. After observing the dying process in our modern life, I extended my teaching and practice into natural conscious dying. So now, when life enters into the passage we call death, I help prepare the dying for as healthy, natural, and pain-free a transition as possible.

Observing dying process in our current modern medical facilities allows me to realize there are valuable things with which Traditional Chinese Medicine can help. This book is my learning path about natural conscious dying that I wish to share with the world. Each case was real, but only the names are fictional to preserve privacy. I try to describe my clinical observation in as much detail as possible so that it may serve as a reference for readers who will encounter a real life conscious dying event. I cannot suppress this passion within for helping people at this important stage of their lives. Conscious dying helps the development of individual cosmic consciousness, of our collective consciousness, and implicitly strengthens the health of our planet. My duty here is to pass this on and bring this intangible ancient wisdom to modern society. In this way I hope to help future generations prevent unseen problems and suffering.

This book generates nothing novel. The ideas presented here all try to remind us of the traditions we already have, though no longer use, or of which we have forgotten the importance. I hope this book will shed some light for you on the ways to help your loved one on the path of natural conscious dying. This transition can leave you with the most beautiful moments and unspoken memories of your life.

INTRODUCTION

Human consciousness refers to an awareness of one's surroundings and internal stimuli coupled with proper reactions to these received stimuli. In Chinese, it is translated as Shen Shi 神识 , equivalent to "conscious awareness". In Chinese culture, 'Shen 神' is this mystical cosmic energy that alchemizes and connects everything in the universe. A similar term can be understood as the cosmic consciousness of the universe. If a life receives Shen (cosmic consciousness), life is lived. If a life loses Shen, then death occurs, according to *Huang Di Nei Jing*, which is also translated as *Yellow Emperor Internal Medicine*, one of the oldest ancient traditional and classic Chinese medicine books.

Consciousness – Soul - Spirit

According to *Yellow Emperor Internal Medicine*, all lives on earth are connected to the Yin Yang of Heaven (cosmic source energies). Shen (cosmic consciousness) is the result of this alchemical transformation between Yin and Yang energies of Heaven (cosmic universe). Thus, consciousness contains a Yang aspect, which many refer to as spirit, and imbues motion and movement with the power of energetic frequencies, called vibrations. Consciousness also has a Yin aspect such as the body of the energy, like the light body. People call it soul. A modern-day metaphor is the action of electricity and light bulbs. Thus, soul is an alternative term for cosmic consciousness that resides in each living individual. It is an energy field, an energetic body that emits certain frequencies of energy. It is a part of universal consciousness (or consciousness of the universe). A good analogy is the existence of the hydrogen atom in the universe. A hydrogen atom contains a proton as Yin aspect and an electron as Yang.

Ethereal Soul and Corporeal Soul

According to Traditional Chinese Medicine (TCM) and Taoist Medicine, Shen from the cosmic source is the cosmic consciousness, and resides inside the human heart. The energetic bodies associated with Shen can enter and leave the human body, and are defined as the ethereal Soul. It is the Yang aspect of the soul, called Hun 魂, which leaves the body after death. The Yin soul is associated with the physical body, as corporeal soul, and is called Po 魄. When people die it remains with the corpse of the deceased.

Taoist tradition believes there are three levels of Yang souls.

The first one is Tian Hun 天魂 (Heaven Hun). It is the main soul that controls human awareness, wisdom, intelligence, knowledge, etc. It can be translated as the astral soul. When the physical body becomes weak, Tian Hun is the soul that leaves the body first.

The second one is called Di Hun 地魂 (Earth soul). This can be translated as subtle soul. Its purpose is to govern feelings of a person, emotional intelligence, analytical abilities, abilities to discriminate between good and bad, kind and evil, ethical judgement, choice of a mate or partner, and feeling of shame or embarrassment.

The third one is called Ming Hun 命魂 (Life soul or Life Hun). It controls the length of a person's life, physical flexibility, and any physical movements and abilities. If it is strong, a person can be in good health and live a long life. If it is weak, a person can develop diseases easily and die at an early age.

Life After Death

According to Chinese folk beliefs, when people die naturally without disease, these three souls will likely depart from the dying person quickly and ascend to higher spiritual realms. Reincarnation is not necessary, but can be their choice if they desire so. When people are weak, these Huns can still depart if given enough time to have a "soul shed" where the dead body is kept for seven days or at least three days in order to allow soul "up-loading".

However, if they are not in good health, people today too often are dying in very different severe conditions. In such cases Life Hun may not be able to depart because it is torn. If people die with no consciousness, Earth Hun will likely not be able to depart. A wandering ghost and reincarnation are then believed to occur.

The Tibetan Book of the Dead offers an abundance of detailed information about the process of reincarnation. In Traditional Chinese culture, complex memorial rituals were carried out and extended over three years. The first 49 days after death include the most vigorous memorial rituals for the deceased. On the final days of the first, third, fifth and seventh week, which means the last day of the odd numbered weeks, the family would go to the burial area to memorialize the departed one. The family would bring food and wine to feed the spirit. This tradition most likely was influenced by the Tibetan Buddhist cultural tradition of the 49-days-of-Bardo stage, an intermediate state between death and reincarnation. These rituals attest to the fact of life after death. The ritual after death is believed to help the souls completely lift from the body and be released without bifurcation. In fact, these practices greatly help the souls reincarnate into a healthy body. The natural dying process was the most common way death happened in old cultures. In those days, this process deeply respected every life.

Nowadays, there are many people dying under the influence of heavy drugs and unnecessary medical procedures. Could this new fashion of dying create unforeseen spiritual problems for this generation and the future ones? Before we go too much farther down that road, let us start a conversation about the healthy way of dying in order for people to be able to consider the impact of the choices they make. As the Taoist saying goes, "Birthing and dying are the two important events of each life, one should not take either lightly."

CHAPTER 1

MY AWAKENING FROM OBSERVING THE DYING

My first observation of a patient's death occurred with a 60 year-old retired nurse. Ann came to me one day with sciatic pain. I decided to put her through several treatments that were successful in treating her condition. She loved my course of treatment and we quickly became friends. A few months later she returned again. This time she had fallen and strained her arm. During this visit Ann confided in me that she was an alcoholic and felt deeply depressed after retiring from the nursing position she had held for 40 years. However, when the time for her third treatment came, she did not show up.

A month passed without a word from her. One Monday while clearing my desk, I noticed her file and decided to give her a call. Ann's husband answered the phone and said, "Ann is dying. She came home last Friday from the hospital and is dying at home." This came as a shock. I could not believe Ann was dying. I really valued the friendship with Ann. I decided to visit her and possibly help her condition. Luckily, Ann's home was really close to my office and it made things easier to visit her.

I found Ann in her living room with an oxygen tube in her nose lying on a hospital bed. "What had happened to Ann?" I asked Ann's husband. He answered quietly, "Ann got pneumonia a month ago and went to the hospital. She had great trouble breathing after receiving some medication and then stopped breathing entirely for a few minutes." He continued, "After that, she was sent to the ICU for life-saving treatment and stayed in the hospital for a month. During that time, she was in and out of a coma. Doctors said her liver had failed due to her alcoholism." I looked at Ann. She had a jaundice-like yellowish pale and withered complexion. Her mouth was open. Her breathing was labored, a gurgling noise coming out of her throat and mouth. I could clearly see the phlegm impairing her breathing. Checking Ann's pulses, her wrist pulse was described in TCM as big, empty, and floating. Her neck pulse was hard to find. It gave me the realization that her Yin-Yang energies were separating.

The wish to help her was coursing through my body and soul. After receiving consent from her husband, I decided to apply my knowledge of acupuncture. I carefully applied needles to her arms. A couple of seconds went by and then Ann's husband noticed her breathing becoming smoother and deeper, and her fingers starting to move. No need to say how happy we both were to see this response. I noticed her breath was now reaching down into her belly. Ann's husband desperately wanted to see a miracle happen. He told me, "A few days ago, Ann opened her eyes when she heard a phone ring and talked on the phone with her friend." I could feel this strong desire on the part of Ann's husband for her to hear and know what was going on around her. However, the morphine kept her in a coma without any sign of consciousness.

I was anxious to continue acupuncture treatments since Ann was responding so favorably, but there was a problem. Ann's sister in-law pulled Ann's husband away and told him that their entire family members and friends had accepted Ann's terminal diagnosis and dying. They had arranged for hospice care to administer morphine every two hours for pain management.

I could sense that some family members and nurses were upset with my coming and trying to help. Ann's husband told me that he acted just like a headless fly, doing whatever other people told him to do. He could not think, could not express his feelings, nor do whatever he realized should be done. He sadly repeated, "All the family members have accepted the fact that Ann is dying. They don't want me to go through this again if Ann cannot live." I was trying to be sincere and told Ann's husband, "I don't want to interrupt your family's decision. If your family would welcome me to help Ann, I would be more than happy to do so." Ann's husband looked at me for a moment and then hugged me. He said, "You are the kindest person I have ever seen." Ann's deep coma from morphine had left her body flaccid, except for her very loud breathing. I gave my blessings to Ann and her husband and left with a very heavy heart.

I walked heavily out of their home. I couldn't get rid of the feeling that there was a far healthier and more compassionate way to support Ann through her inevitable dying process. A big concern arose in me, as with heavy steps I made my way towards my car. My fear was if this would be the standard way for dying in the future, we, as spiritual beings, would be overlooked and many of us might end up with drugs when we could not speak for ourselves. A natural way of supporting dying needs to be available in the future!

This event became a turning point for me to pay attention to the subject of conscious dying and death. My teaching in TCM schools and clinical practice started to extend to human conscious dying and death.

CHAPTER 2

DYING
WITH SICKNESS

Ann's dying left a lasting impression on me. It was my very first experience of this kind. My second observation of a dying patient happened with the mother of one of my students. She was an 87-year-old Vietnamese lady who had suffered an ischemic stroke three weeks prior to her death. I shall refer to my student as Vhin and to his mother as Maiy. Maiy was found unconscious one morning at her home. The family called 911 and Maiy was taken to the emergency room and admitted to ICU. When Vhin asked me to visit his mother after my class, I gladly accepted. We went there only to find Maiy in a coma. Multiple tests and a brain scan determined that her brain was severely damaged. The reality set in - recovery would not be possible. She had been in ICU for a couple of days.

Except for feeling cold all the time, especially in her legs, for several weeks prior to the stroke, Maiy had been healthy and had no known chronic illnesses. Now she was connected to machines for life support in the ICU and had a big breathing tube in her mouth. Maiy was a thin person. Her face was a yellowish pale white with a glossy shine. I checked her wrist pulse which felt like a very fine thread with little pulsation. It presented her vital energy being extremely low. Her body felt warm and legs showed some edema, likely caused by the great amount of IV fluids being infused into her body. I applied a couples of acupressure points on her arms. Her eyeballs started to move. I encouraged Vhin to massage his mother and apply some acupressure techniques. As Vhin touched his mother, I saw her respond. Maiy stretched her arms and legs, and made chewing motions, but with the breathing tube in her mouth and down into her throat, she couldn't verbalize any sound, release tension orally, or release dryness of her mouth. I felt sad to see Maiy like this. The family was facing the decision of whether or not to remove the hospital life support within three days. The question of who would care for Maiy if she were taken home troubled them, and so they hurriedly decided to leave Maiy where she was.

Surprisingly, when oxygen support was removed, Maiy was able to breathe on her own. Family members were taking turns watching Maiy overnight. Vhin stayed the most nights watching his mother he noticed nurses coming into the room a few times and attempting to inject morphine into his mother. Vhin's unease grew and finally he refused them, "My mother already looks peaceful. She has no signs of any pain or discomfort. Why does she need morphine?" He challenged them, raising his voice. Once the nurses left and Vhin was able to spend the time alone with his mother. He kept up with massages to comfort his mother whenever he felt necessary.

On the fifth day after removing life support, Maiy died peacefully. That day, Vhin had visited his mother before coming to my class. Right before Vhin was going to leave Maiy, she opened her eyes and looked at him. Vhin was so happy! He told his mother that he wanted to take a picture of her. Maiy seemed to understand him and looked at his camera. Vhin left the hospital and came to class. Ten minutes after the class began, he received a call and left. The hospital called telling Vhin his mother had passed. The following week, Vhin shared his emotions and his story with me. He was just so happy he had been able to take a picture of his mother a moment before her passing. It was a precious moment for Vhin because his mom never woke up and had no verbal communication ever since going to ICU. It was a great comfort for Vhin to have this moment with his mother opening her eyes. Vhin's effort to keep the morphine away from his mother likely made this possible.

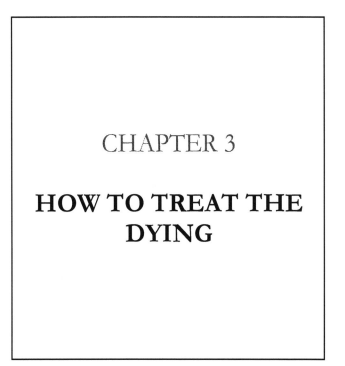

CHAPTER 3

HOW TO TREAT THE DYING

I n today's world, discussing death and dying often makes people feel cold, depressed, and fearful. It's so common for people to associate death with something negative. Even hearing the word "death" can send chills through the body or invoke sadness. It does not have to be this way. People can generate and cherish a new understanding of death. Death can be seen as a life passage, a beautiful event and the start of a new life, just like the birth of a child. It is a process of the revitalization of a soul. Humans can depart from this world with strong bonds, compassion, humility, wisdom, love, and respect for each other. Buddhism and many traditional cultures alike teach and practice this pathway for a compassionate life transition. The wisdom of these cultural and spiritual traditions has been passed on by participating in and witnessing the process of death and dying.

My mother is an authentic example of someone gaining knowledge and cultural wisdom through life experiences shared with her parents and elders. Here allow me to firstly describe a childhood story of my mother learning about life, death, and spirit-soul.

Soul Calling (Jiao Hun) is one of the Chinese folk traditions that was practiced very commonly in the old time. It is believed that souls can fly out of the body when a person is in physical trauma, like a car accident, a fall from a high place, or the body being poisoned. Before the dying person has fully completed their transition, soul calling is used to bring the spirit back to the person. When my mother was about seven years old, she saved her own mother's life with experiencing a Soul Calling.

It was a winter night. Her father was working out of town. My mom slept in a room with her mother and her infant brother. My mother was awakened by the noise from her mother retching and vomiting. She shook her mother vigorously, but her mother did not respond. Because my mother slept near the window, they were certain she wasn't affected by the carbon monoxide from the coal they burned for heating. Neither was her brother who slept inside the cover. At that period of time, people still lived in an old fashion way, a brick stove built to connect with a big brick bed for a family to sleep on. In winter time, coal was used for heating.

My mother, still only a little girl, got out of bed, ran out to knock on her uncle's door, and called out for people to help. Many adults came to help. One grand uncle was trying to revive grandma's consciousness by pressing the middle point of philtrum (Du 26, Ren Zhong), the area below the nostrils and above upper lip. My mother was asked to get up on the roof to call her mother's spirit. She stood on the roof and called her mother loudly, asking her spirit to come back, "Mother, please come back, please don't leave us. We can't live without you. Mom please come back…" It was very early in the morning, her voice penetrated the whole village. So after a few minutes, with acupressure, physical touch, and soul-calling, grandmother regained consciousness and was alive once again. This was the story of how my mom saved her mother's life. I loved my grandma dearly during my childhood and she lived to 70+ years of age.

Every individual is influenced by their own culture and spiritual beliefs. My belief, as a traditional Chinese medical doctor, is that the dying process should be as conscious as possible, and as natural as possible. Chinese culture and traditional Chinese medicine carry a very deep understanding of human life, death and dying, and life after death. There is so much people can learn and benefit from this wisdom.

The growth of modern science and technology has been so rapid and invasive that we as a species have lost sight of the importance of learning from our elders, parents, grandparents and ancestors. Gaps between generations become obvious. Elders have many beneficial things to offer younger generations. Thus, human culture is nurtured and expanded through this invaluable sharing of knowledge and wisdom. If we part too far from our elders, we may lose the heart and wisdom of our culture.

In the following chapters I will present and describe examples of healthy, positive deaths. The first story is the actually a good-death story of my own mother's grandmother, my great grandmother. The second and third stories of natural conscious dying are from my clinical cases.

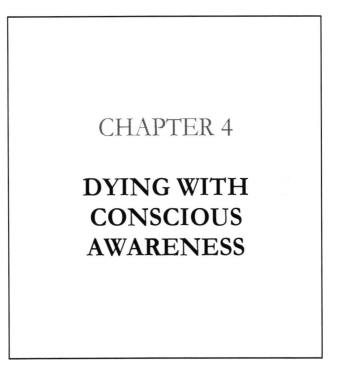

CHAPTER 4

DYING WITH CONSCIOUS AWARENESS

My dear parents are healthy and active and currently live with me. My mother is 76 and my father is approaching 83 at this writing. My mother's mind is sharp and she can recall many detailed memories and stories from her life. She grew up in the countryside in China surrounded by thousands of years of accumulated and respected, highly traditional culture. What is considered a good or a bad dying experience in Chinese culture? I will bring you the case of my great grandmother's death, this time through a story my mother shared with me about the death of her father's mother. I will call her GG.

GG was considered a shamanic woman in her day. She was intelligent, quick and alert. She was also a country midwife and a doctor. Since in those days no schools formally taught traditional Chinese medicine, her uncle had taught her Chinese medicine. GG helped many people and saved many lives. She was helping women with infertility issues, headaches, painful menstruation, leucorrhea, uterine fibroids, trauma injuries, etc. She also treated infants and children. People came by horse-drawn wagon from surrounding villages and beyond to see her, often bartering goods such as cottons, clothes or harvests in exchange for her services.

When I was little, I attended her 65th birthday celebration. There were so many merry people, most of whom I didn't know. It made me laugh to see them kneeling down before my great-grandma. I grew up in the city, and these old traditions were foreign to me. Watching for a while, I could see the pure sincerity of their actions. Some were bowing so low they knocked their head on the floor. It was a complete mystery to me why these guests would do that before my great-grandma. Today, I understand they did it because GG had helped many people conceive, bear, and deliver children, and because she had saved many lives.

"How did your grandma die?" I asked my mother. She answered, "When my grandma was closer to her nineties, she slowly started to feel increasingly tired. She stopped working when she just couldn't continue anymore. However, she was able to hear and see without any problem." My mother told me that GG rarely got sick and was in good health until the very day she died. Two weeks before GG died, she said to her husband, "I've had enough of my life here, it is my time to leave." She washed herself, put on clean clothes, and lay on her bed without eating. Families asked her if they could bring a doctor to see her, but she refused all the suggestions about taking medicine, seeing doctors, or eating food. She simply said, "My time has arrived, it is time to return to heaven now. I have no desire to eat anything." Respectfully, GG's family let her quietly and peacefully rest. Members of both close and extended families were notified. During this period, GG asked for particular people to visit her. My mother was one of them. GG had something to straighten out with my mother. When my mother was a child, GG had accused her of stealing a pair of jade bracelets. Eventually, GG found out it was another girl who had stolen the bracelets. Now, on her death bed, GG wanted my mother to forgive her. As my mother told this story, she was happy. With joy, she said, "When I was little, I felt there was something wrong between me and my grandma. I felt she didn't quite like me, I didn't know why. I thought it might have been due to my being naughty, but we never resolved that until this moment of truth."

"When my grandma told me what that problem was all about right before she died, I finally understood what had happened, and I was very happy that she had asked me to forgive her." My mother continued. "When old people are dying, they try to clear up things with living people, they don't like to carry these things with them, and want to go with a clean and clear heart, with no worries or guilt." It is something so inherent to all human beings.

And what was the last request my great-grandma ever made? Her last request was to have a bowel movement. That happened a couple hours before her last breath. Her husband carried her and held her from the back to let her sit on a pot. She was awake and aware. Shortly afterwards, she passed away at night. GG died quietly and peacefully. During the fourteen-day transition of her dying into her death, GG was drinking only water. She had no incontinence of urine or stool. Following her dying, GG's body was kept on her bed until the next afternoon. At sunset, her body was moved to a newly built "soul shed" (Ling Peng, 灵棚). Family, friends, and neighbors helped to build this "soul shed" and decorate it with lots of white cloth. Everything was covered with white cloth indicating the purity. After the last breath, it is believed a soul continues to separate from the physical body and moved to a purer place, or heaven. GG's body was kept there for seven days from the date of death according to the local traditions until it was finally buried.

According to the village custom, if the person who died was old, a big celebration would be offered. The family would host an opera singer, dancing, and plays for several days. But in cases where a person was young and succumbing to an untimely death from disease, accident, homicide, or suicide, there would be no singing or dancing. Those funerals happened quietly and people mostly felt sad. GG's natural death is considered the good way to die in Chinese culture. It is called "Shuo Zhong Zheng Qin" (寿终正寝), meaning a person dies at the designated time without any illness. It is one of the five fortunes a human should have, according to *Sang Shu* (《尚书》), one of the oldest historical books in China.

CHAPTER 5

NATURAL CONSCIOUS DYING WITH TRADITIONAL CHINESE MEDICINE

The following story of conscious dying comes from one of my clinical cases. I was using acupuncture and moxibustion to provide help for a terminally ill patient so that he could have a peaceful life transition. I will refer to this person as Jay and to his son as Tim. Jay had a brain tumor.

Jay, a man in his early sixties, had been diagnosed with a brain tumor and cancer six months before, and was being actively treated in a hospital. At the end of his radiation treatments, his body collapsed. He sadly suffered extreme ribcage distention, pain and bloating, along with neck pain on the right side. He died with liver failure at the end.

I first treated Jay at home one month before he died. Jay looked emaciated. He had little muscle tone and scarce fatty tissue. His hands and feet were cold. His skin color was yellowish pale. He was urinating frequently, however, bowel movements were difficult. Further observations of TCM diagnosis, Jay's tongue was red and cracked with no coating. His pulse was thin and weak. Despite all of this, Jay was in good spirits, and showed a bit of humor. His mind seemed clear. He was polite, gentle, and positive.

My diagnosis for Jay was that he was both Yin and

Yang deficient, as well as Qi and blood deficient. It was apparent that he had been administered many medications. Jay's physical condition was severely depleted going through his course of treatments. Talking about his condition, he told me that just five months before he was as strong as a cow. He couldn't believe how things had worsened so quickly. After the first acupuncture treatment which I applied, Jay felt energy returning to his body. A week later, I gave him another acupuncture treatment and Jay said he felt very good after the treatment. He was able to take a walk outdoor and do some stretches.

On Wednesday, 3 days before his passing away, I went to treat Jay at his home again. It was five days after his last radiation treatment. Jay was so tired he could barely get up. The right side of his neck and shoulder was in extreme pain. His liver side of the ribcage was exceptionally distended, and hurt. His ankle was also swollen. He had been lying in bed and finding it very hard to move. In addition to his scheduled medication, Jay was taking pain medication every four hours. I observed a drastic decline in his wellness compared with the last time I had seen him. Acupuncture seemed to effectively reduce his pain. On Thursday, Tim took his father for a blood draw. The following day, Jay's doctor came to his home and told the family Jay's liver was failing and he needed not continue with his medication. Jay slipped into a non-responsive state later that evening.

Emergency Call Received

On Saturday night, I received news from Tim that his father was in a coma and he needed my help. It was almost 11:00 pm when I reached their home and found Jay surrounded by his son, his wife of Thai descent, and Tim's friend who is a registered nurse, Ida. Jay was lying on the bed in a coma, but was brushing his arms downward on his belly repeatedly, and moaning silently, without a word. Tim told me that Jay had received one small dose of morphine, but it seemed to quiet him for only one hour. My friend and his father Jay believed in the natural process of dying, and Tim wanted it for Jay. At this moment, Jay was surrounded with great love, care, focus and attention from all of us, but he wasn't aware of any of this, and his body was cold. His eyes were closed, with no movement. He was continually moaning and brushing his arms downwards.

I quickly applied acupuncture needles to his body. Within minutes of receiving acupuncture needles, Jay started to wave his arms and touch his body, seeming to find himself. A few minutes later, his eyes started to roll and move. He tried to open them. Finally, he did open his eyes several times, looking to see who I was, but, there was no glimmer of light in the eyeballs. The moaning reduced. He started saying "Far, far, far..." He had not spoken this before the treatment. I gave Jay an herbal tea and Ida helped feed him with a spoon. As the spoon touched his lips, Jay opened his mouth and managed to swallow. He responded to the feeding very well without much problem of swallowing the tea. He took only two or three times and then stopped.

Meanwhile, as I used a moxa box on his lower body and bottom of his feet, Jay started to move his body and left arm with greater strength. His consciousness was trying to command his body again.

Jay's Spirit Returning

Smoke from the moxa filled up the room. Within 10 minutes of taking the tea, Jay woke up with a big, beautiful smile. A look of pure happiness graced his face. It was the type of expression you see on a baby's face. He opened his eyes. Now, Jay's gaze was clear with a glimmer of light inside. It was as if he had awakened from a deep sleep. He said loudly and clearly, "Amazing room, amazing room..." He moved his arms, brushing his head. Although smoky from the moxa, the room felt pleasant. We were surprised Jay had awakened. I instructed Tim to ask his father if he felt warm or cold. Jay didn't respond to these questions, but instead repeated, "Amazing room, amazing room…amazing room". I knew he wasn't in the same space as us. Then I instructed Tim to ask him again, "Do you want to drink some water?" This time he replied, "Yes." Ida fed him water through a straw. Afterward, Jay kept saying, "Amazing room, amazing room…" Then his voice became fainter. He returned to the dream state, and kept saying "Far…far…far" loudly.

Spirit Leaving The Earth Realm

I kept moxa on his legs and feet as acupuncture needles were placed in his arms and legs. After a while, I decided to add a few needles on his head as well. As I did this, Jay murmured, "Father, father, father…" Then, "Forever, forever, forever…" I was surprised to hear what Jay said, wondering what it meant. Tim and Ida returned to the room after a short break. I had them put a big plastic pad beneath Jay's back and bottom area to catch any urination or defecation that might be released. About 10 minutes passed and Jay burst into another radiant smile right before transitioning into throat breathing and saying, "Grandma, my family…", three times in a very weak voice. His wife took over at this moment. Jay changed to quick throat breathing just afterwards, then came long exhalations from the mouth only. There was no inhalation. Jay's wife cried quietly, aware it would be her husband's last moment in life. Within one minute, he blew out one last big breath. His eyes were open. His body's vibration from breathing ceased completely. In that same instant, I felt as if a kind of wave had passed through my body. I looked at the clock on the wall, it was almost 12:57 a.m. I knew Jay's soul and spirit had just left his body. This was the very final moment of his transition into death.

I asked them to remove the plastic pad from underneath his bottom, and dress him. The plastic pad held his final, dark urine. There was no stool. Everything went smoothly and peacefully. There was no mess left or unpleasant situation created. Dressed in his favorite clothes, Jay was laid out on his bed. He remained there undisturbed through the night. When I returned with flowers the next morning, Jay's face looked relaxed and he wore a shy smile. I detected no expression of discomfort or sadness on his face. His transition was complete and beautiful.

Unseen Grateful Lights

The family wanted to follow the Thai Buddhist funeral tradition. Jay's conscious death experience set a positive tone for his funeral. Three Thai monks came and chanted during the ceremonies. It was very crowded inside his home that day. I went outside to watch my daughter play with a little girl. A few of Jay's relatives were also outside on the grass. While standing there, I gradually felt a swirling energy in front of my heart chakra, the energy center in front of the heart. It was a feeling of peace, happiness, and joy being directed at me. Placing my awareness on this energy, a message came to my mind. I believe it was Jay's spirit, or at least his spirit's guide coming to thank me. This swirling energy lasted for a few minutes. I had had this energy-swirling experience once before. It was during a guided meditation with a Taoist Qi Gong master and I was able to interpret the message I received at that amazing moment. Jay's funeral was a wonderful experience. Jay's wife and son recovered from their initial sadness very quickly and both looked very contented. A healthy dying event can affect people's lives in very positive and amazing ways.

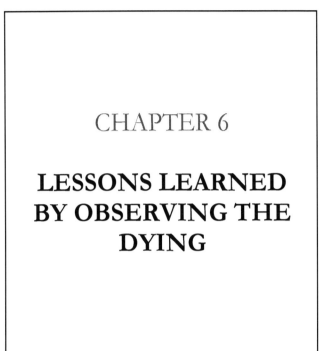

CHAPTER 6

LESSONS LEARNED BY OBSERVING THE DYING

Before focusing on Jay's case and subsequently summarizing the stages of the dying process according to Chinese traditional culture, I would like to offer concluding remarks on these four cases I have presented so far.

Case 1

Ann was dying in a deep coma and had received morphine injections. Her breathing responded to acupuncture treatment, but due to the choice made by her family, Ann's dying was under the influence of morphine. This unnatural way of dying raises serious concerns because we do not know the full spiritual or physical effects of these unnatural drugs on the human soul.

Case 2

Maiy had aged naturally to 87 years of age. She had been in a good health and had no significant health conditions. Unfortunately, when Maiy was found in a coma, she was sent to ICU care. After the medical tests concluded, it was determined there was no hope of saving her life. The hospital removed life support and then injected morphine. Fortunately, Maiy's son, Vhin, was able to do some massage on her legs and arms. Maiy was able to breathe on her own for five days and the injecting of morphine was kept to a minimum. Maiy could open her eyes before dying, her spirit saying its final goodbye to this world. Luckily, her son captured the precious moment. For the most part, Maiy remained in a coma once she reached the ICU so there was no further communication between her and her family. The anesthesia Maiy received prevented her consciousness from being awakened.

Case 3

Should we consider GG a spiritual practitioner in the dying process? She was so conscious and aware of her mind and soul that when her time to die came, she recognized it and accepted it with no hesitation. She was supported and surrounded by her loving family, following the old tradition. During her dying process, she was able to forgive and to allow those whom she had offended to forgive her. She was mindful and present. Her death was peaceful and conscious, an example of healthy dying.

Since ancient times, dying old was viewed as proof of life fulfilled and completed. It was considered a good fortune for the soul. GG tried to clear all unresolved karma before her soul left the human world. In Chinese culture, we believe this brings a free, fresh start for the soul in the next life, brimming with positive energy for everyone involved. Just so natural!

A human death needs not necessarily be associated with disease, nor always occur in a medical facility. Traditional Chinese Medicine teaches us that there is a very real and available possibility for people to experience their dying process with mind, body and spirit intact. This is considered the good way of dying in Traditional Chinese culture and it is still respected in many areas of China today. TCM's mission is to follow the Taoist teachings of the importance of living in harmony with nature and with all souls involved.

As we can see, there are big differences between Maiy and GG. The commonality is that both were healthy throughout their entire lives. This leads me to an important question, how can we, in this culture, help people who are as healthy as Maiy avoid dying with hospital trauma? How can we enable people who are as healthy as Maiy have the late life transformation as in the case of GG? These are my main interests regarding elderly alternative care. Just as there is a healthy way to live, there is a healthy way to die. Families must not believe that removing life support is their only option in the final stages of treating terminally ill loved ones.

Case 4

Jay was fortunate to have a good and beautiful, morphine-free, natural and completely conscious dying process supported by both acupuncture and moxibustion. Jay's life unfortunately ended due to the progression of the disease combined with the deleterious effects of pharmaceutical drugs. His vital energy and blood were severely damaged and the physical body became extremely thin and weak at the end, so that his spirit and soul were not supported by his physical body anymore. A life thus was ended.

Modern medicine in general has not yet been able to measure the spirit or soul because spirit and soul are not of the material world. In fact, this significant lack of spiritual and emotional support in this medical treatment model of the dying process can harm the soul or even hasten death. I strongly suggest that change is needed! The story of Jay's dying lights a hope for positive change in the future.

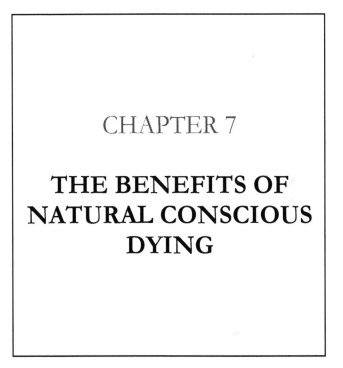

CHAPTER 7

THE BENEFITS OF NATURAL CONSCIOUS DYING

There is so much we can learn from overseeing the journey of Jay's soul transition. During his last hours on earth, his spirit fighting for life, despite his bodily functions being severely worn down and failing. Jay's consciousness was able to be revived with the treatment by acupuncture and moxibustion. The TCM treatment gave his physical body an energetic boost so that his spirit, his consciousness, was able to determine its next path.

Until his last breath, Jay was able to communicate with the people around him. His body's dying process went smoothly with no signs of discomfort. There was happiness, joy, and beauty in the process. Jay was encircled by, and held with, love, care and compassion. Most importantly, his soul's next journey was fully supported. Jay's spirit returned to him and he was able to wake up and speak aloud "Amazing room, amazing room…" In our Chinese tradition, this phenomenon is called "Hui Guang Fan Zhao" (回光返照). "Hui" means, "returned, back home". "Guang" means, "light." "Fan Zhao", means, "shining back." It understands as "returned light shines back."

A very similar phenomenon is reported in Osis & Haroldsson's book *At the Hour of Death*, (1972).

Researchers successfully collated compelling evidence that suggests we, as conscious beings, do survive physical death, and I believe that cases of "post-mortem existence" have occurred. "Hui Guang Fan Zhao" (回光返照) is a well-known common phenomenon in traditional Chinese culture as a sign of dying. Taoist tradition says the astral soul, "Tian Hun", is coming to bring the subtle soul, "Di Hun", back to the heavenly realm. When these two souls successfully bond together out of a body, it gives a chance to reach to a higher Heaven realm. Another common expression for the spirit leaving a body is Ling Hun Chu Qiao (灵魂出窍), which translates as "souls bursting out of orifices" that is observed in dying people.

Jay spoke to those people he could see around him. He expressed "Father, father, father, forever, forever, forever…," suggesting to me that his spirit was flying away from his body and he was saying goodbye to his son. He continued his travels and reached the spirit realm where he met and joined his family. That happened at the very end, when he surprisingly said "My grandma, my family." three times. Jay's final words brought vast comfort to his survivors. It was a great relief for them to believe he had been welcomed by his ancestors at the very last moment of his spirit leaving his body. This is a tremendous benefit of dying consciously. Could it be that Jay had really reunited with his deceased relatives and forefathers in another dimension, a spirit realm, of which we humans are normally unaware? We may not be able to unequivocally answer this question, but what matters is what the family believes.

In traditional Chinese culture as in other ancient cultures people learned about dying and death by experiencing death rituals as part of life. Death was about being consciously present at the time of this transition. The rituals were intended to help all those associated with the transition. Death was culturally ritualized, rather than considered a medical event which is often hidden away from people's view. People who grew up with such similar ancient traditions, no matter in which culture, learned about the dying process from their everyday life, just as my mother had. My mother had been immersed in the details of the dying process and rituals throughout her life. She learned through those rituals and her culture, not through a medical system.

Sadly, in modern life, we have been losing these precious traditions of learning from our elders.

Elders have so much wisdom and life experiences to pass on to younger generations. That is how culture is formed, deepened and treasured. That is how people realized the existence of eternal life, souls, life after death and reincarnation. It is not possible for people to develop these concepts in one or two generations. It takes many life times, generations, and accumulated cultural heritage of direct experiences of life-death transition to generate such wisdom.

The purpose of helping our elders to have such healthy peaceful dying and death transitions is to benefit their soul's growth and ascension. Overall, such transformation would benefit human societies and human consciousness collectively.

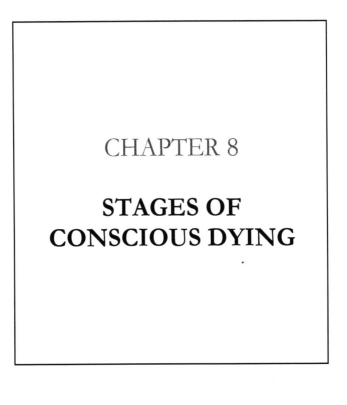

CHAPTER 8

STAGES OF
CONSCIOUS DYING

Having offered my reflections on each of the cases cited, I would now like to turn my focus to the stages of dying as taught by traditional Chinese culture. I argue that a person who succeeds in dying consciously, will experience five stages that are externally visible. Here are the common phenomena as exemplified in Jay's experience:

1.   *Before-coma phenomenon:*

Jay experienced a lack of appetite, diminished interest in his surroundings, no desire to eat or drink, sleepiness all the time, lassitude, weakness, and feeling cold. According to TCM, this indicates his life fire (Yang) was in decline.

2.   *During-coma state:*

Jay became unconscious with no visible response to his surroundings, with shallow breathing and with exhalations longer than inhalations. And after his consciousness was revived with TCM, there was an increase in his body movements, eye movements resumed -- he opened his eyes -- and he was able to swallow liquid.

3.   *Life-returning phenomenon:*

Jay suddenly woke up with a beautiful smile on his face, and was talking. Life seemed to return. In some cases, though not in Jay's, hunger may be revived and patients wish to eat food. This phenomenon may last for a few minutes or for hours. In Chinese culture, this well-known phenomenon is called "Returned Light Shining Back" (Hui Guang Fan Zhao, 回光返照). Finally, speech may return as it happened with Jay repeating "forever" and "goodbye" quite often.

4.   Lost internal Qi phenomenon:

Consciousness may be lost again in this stage as we saw in Jay falling back into a coma. His breathing grew shallower with long exhalations. This stage may be long or short. A last bowel movement or urination can happen at this time. Afterward, the dying person may express seeing somebody close to them who pre-deceased them, indicating that the soul/spirit has now reached the heavenly realm.

5.   Throat breathing to one last Qi blowing phenomenon:

In this final stage, breathing ceases. Here we saw Jay experience rapid exhalation through the throat. He blew out air a few times from the mouth and then had one final, long exhalation. Following this, breathing ceased completely.

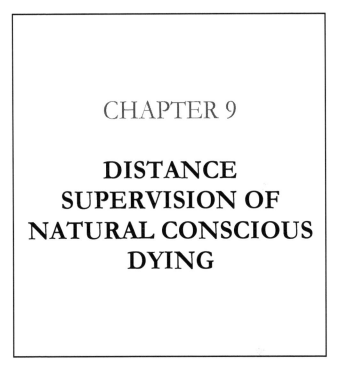

CHAPTER 9

DISTANCE SUPERVISION OF NATURAL CONSCIOUS DYING

This is a case of the long distance supervision of a family member taking care of their loved one through natural conscious dying. This experience greatly deepened my understanding of the significance of natural conscious dying.

In late April 2015, a year after helping Jay with his conscious dying, I received a call from one of my closest friends, Terry, who was living on the east coast. His mother, Julie, was diagnosed with late-stage both lung and pancreatic cancer. She was deemed a patient with no possibility of treatment. After being hospitalized for ten days, hospital doctors determined that it was time for her to receive hospice care. I encouraged my friend Terry to bring his mom home for her last days. At home, she could receive family love, care, and natural healing. I could advise him about his mother's condition.

Julie returned home with extreme physical weakness. She could not get herself out of the vehicle. She had to be carried out of the car, placed in a wheel chair and wheeled into the house by Terry and his dad. Julie was given medications prescribed by the hospice doctor that included four types of drugs: strong pain-control medications, anti-nausea drugs, stool softening pills, and anti-blood clotting drugs.

Three days went by, and Julie's energy and spirit were rapidly getting weaker, leaving her with barely any appetite. I advised Terry to stop all the pain medications and apply heating pads to keep her body warm and alleviate pain. It may sound surprising, but her pain was successfully reduced by only using heating pads without any pain medication. She was in and out of sleep, but remained conscious and was able to carry on short conversations with family and friends. Occasionally, she drank some carrot juice or water. Terry and his dad stayed by her side 24 hours a day every day. I was also on 24-hour call for Terry if he needed my advice about what Julie should eat and drink, and how to control any symptoms if they came up. At the same time, I was involved in treating my patients in my clinic in Marin, California. Both Terry's and my initial focus was to see if there was a possibility of prolonging Julie's life. We were trying to keep her energy strong, making her as comfortable as possible, while trying to keep her consciously awake by reducing the use of pain drugs to none. This succeeded. Julie was able to drink some ginger tea, carrot juice and rice soup. She received a great deal of loving care from her sons and husband. Things went smoothly with her, and she had no complaints about any physical discomfort.

Massage to Relieve Coughing

On the fourth night Julie started to experience difficulty breathing and started to cough, I instructed Terry to use a few acupuncture points to do acupressure. Terry was able to remain calm and focused, giving his mom a massage, coaching her to focus on her breathing and to try to relax by keeping her breath slow and deep. Dedicating himself to this mission, Terry was finally able to relax his mom and the cough was stopped. After this, however, another issue emerged: Julie told Terry her feet were itching. So Terry began to massage Julie's feet with cream. While performing the massage, Terry noticed his mom appearing more at ease and calm. The spasms of the diaphragm were also softened. A few hours later, Julie's cough became worse again. Despite the initial use of acupressure points which seemed to have failed, Terry started to actively massage his mom's abdominal area along the diaphragm. Familiar with Reiki energy healing, he kept sending Qi (life force energy) to the diaphragm area to relax the muscles. He kept massaging until his mom was once again completely absorbed in a rhythmic breathing with no spasms -- this, despite her breathing still being labored.

Unknown and Doubting

Since the afternoon of the fifth day, Julie was in a

deep non-responsive sleep or coma. In the evening Terry and his friend engaged in Sanskrit chanting for his mom. It was close to midnight when Terry called me and expressed discouragement that had crept in while watching his mom in a coma-like state. Terry felt very saddened because he understood this was a sign of his mom on her path to dying.

Would that be it? His mother was going to die without wakening up ever again? Apparently, I knew it was a critical moment for Terry's mother, so I stayed in my office that night. I centered my energy, meditated a few minutes and kept positive thoughts, assuring Terry what he had done was a great job for his mom even though she was going to die. I assured him that, regardless of whether his mom would really die soon or live a few moments more, the best thing for her was that she stayed at home surrounded by the loving care of her husband and sons instead of nurses. That was a big blessing for his mom during her last days. I assured him that everything he had undertaken was a great deed which any person should do for their parents. This kind of respect is greatly valued in many cultures and is somehow greatly underestimated in western societies.

Even though I reassured Terry about this, my own

mind began to raise some doubts and worries. I was overwhelmingly exhausted going through all those days positioned on the front line of supervising Terry in the care of his mother during her last days. It was as if I had been there with him, in his mind and body, all the time. That late evening, after talking to Terry, I sat down. Being quiet for a few minutes, I started pondering whether I should be doing this again for others or not? Is it worth investing so much energy and emotions in trying to help others in this end-of-life work? People still go into a coma and finally die! The truth was, at that moment, I wasn't sure what would happen with Julie. Would Julie die now? Would all of our efforts just lead her into a deep, deep coma and – that was it?

And it was at this moment that I started to feel the same disappointment as Terry. As I witnessed, family members who were not ready for their loved one's death, were desperately prone to expect miracles, longing for more time. Regardless of these thoughts, I could sense Terry was sadder and more despairing than I was. I decided to send out an email with encouragement and support for him and my blessings to Julie. At the end of the email I expressed the Buddha's blessing, "Ah Mi Tuo Fuo" ("May infinity light, wisdom and longevity shine on you"). The clock was showing 1:00 a.m.

Overpowered by the web of these thoughts, by exhaustion and worry, I fell asleep.

Spirit Shed the Light through My Dream

I slept through the night, my sleep plagued by many dreams. As the night was coming to a close and early morning was approaching, I woke up after a very unusual dream which was absolutely vivid and clear. The message from this dream was incredible and almost unbelievable. It cleared up my doubts and despair. I felt it validated the work we had done for Julie. This dream provided me with so much energy and happiness the next day and washed off all the fatigue and disappointment.

The dream experience was incredible. Readers must be wondering why I was so affected by this dream. It was not a simple dream! I believe it was a message from spirits living in a higher realm. I will share with you the details of my dream in the next chapter. Here, let me continue with the story of Julie's death and the impact it had on her family and my work.

When I woke up from this dream, my mind repeated this message like a mantra, "your help pushed her out of the MUD..., pushed her out of the MUD, pushed her out of the MUD..." It seemed if I didn't chant it, I would lose this important message. I felt so excited and had a strong urge to share this unusual dream with Terry. I turned on my phone …

Julie's Consciousness Returned

As soon as my phone was on, Terry's texted message popped up right at the moment, "My mom woke up this morning with lots of foam and greenish mucus in her mouth. I helped clean up her mouth. Her voice is weak but she can talk." I texted Terry about the dream. I tried to briefly share the excitement and show him the validation of the work we had been doing together. Also, I asked Terry to encourage his mom on my behalf and to simply tell her something nice, like how beautiful she was. I used an expression, "She's going to be as beautiful as the Quan Yin Statue." This day, as it was recorded in Terry's diary, Julie's facial complexion became pinkish, she was conscious and lucid. The jaundice yellow color on her skin and eyes was reduced. This dream conveyed to me so many meaningful messages. Some messages I could easily understand, but most messages were beyond my scope of knowledge. However, the spiritual guidance from my dreams was not an unusual thing to me. I sincerely believed a higher spirit communicated to me about the doubts I had. After waking up from this dream, all of the exhaustion, physical tiredness, confusion and worries were wiped away. I felt refreshed and happy, and most notably, I received a strong encouragement for working on natural conscious dying for people in need, and helping soul ascensions.

Relayed by Terry:
The Last Day Being with Mom

"On the 6th day, Dad woke me around 7:30 a.m. and left to do errands, leaving Mom alone with me. I figured I would talk to Mom just as I always had. I said, "Good morning, Mom." Mom responded, "Good morning, Terry." I was so surprised to see Mom conscious again. Mom had a yellow green mucus and foam in her mouth that had been drooling from her mouth onto a paper towel which dad had placed under her chin. I cleaned her face and mouth. I offered Mom a sip of water which she drank easily. I began talking to Mom explaining to her why Dad and my brother were not here. I asked Mom if she recalled her brother coming here last night or if she remembered us playing her gospel music. She said no. Apparently, last night she was in a deep sleep, unconsciousness.

I did not know for how long Mom would be conscious, so I first called Dad, then sent a text message to Joy, and then called other family members to let them know Mom was conscious again. Mom even spoke to her younger sister Jackie. Mom told Jackie that she loved her. During this time, I told Mom that I loved her and how much I appreciated all the things she had done for me. I played Mom's favorite gospel songs for her, could see how moved she was, she was crying with love and devotion for God. I told her to go to the white light when she would be able to see it. I told her to remember to surrender her entire being to Jesus and God. After that, Dad returned home and talked to Mom. Mom complained of her feet itching. Dad offered to use a warm bubble spa on Mom's feet to wash them and finally they stopped itching. Dad commented that Mom's eyes were not as yellow, and that her face had more color, not as pale as before. Mom's condition was stable throughout the day, yet at some point she had difficulty breathing. Dad was panicked and gave her a small dosage of morphine. In my opinion, it was not a good idea to do so. Luckily, Mom's consciousness was not affected. Later, she could not sip fluid anymore. I stayed up with Mom deep into the night. Her breathing became very labored again. I went to sleep at 4:40 a.m. Dad woke me in the morning at 9:13 a.m. Dad said the time of Mom's passing was getting close. I checked on Mom's hands and feet. They still had some warmth. Mom was in a labored breathing pattern, but not as laborious as she had been earlier in the evening. I said good morning to Mom. I could see that Mom was making an effort to respond, but could not. She lifted her head up a little as if she would say something, but she was unable to voice anything. My brother was next to her. I understood this was the last moment, I said "I love you, mom. I love you very much." I played mom's favorite gospel songs: Amazing Grace[1], How Great Thou Art[2], 'Shine, Jesus, Shine[3].

While playing How Great Thou Art everyone became silent in a reverential worship of God. I could see Mom was very moved…that the Holy Spirit was coming into her as she opened up to God. I cried silently with joyfulness from witnessing the light of God, the Grace of God, the beauty of this precious moment. I was crying with an intense love for and devotion to God. Mom lifted her head a few times and her body and breathing perked up with more energy. My aunt Jackie, my dad, my brother and I were all present around Mom, witnessing this beautiful moment.

When "Shine, Jesus, Shine" stopped playing, we just remained silent, observing Mom and letting the mind be still. I noticed that Mom's breathing was growing softer and softer, with less and less energy with each breath. I checked her hands. Her finger tips were getting very cold even with my having held her hand for a while. I told everyone Mom's breathing had changed, becoming very soft. Then I got up to check her feet. I sat down in the chair facing Mom. Her feet were cold too. Jackie sat down at Mom's side, holding her hand. Right after checking Mom's feet, Mom had watery blood streaming out of her nose. Perhaps about two-thimble-full worth from each nose. I told Dad Mom is dying right now. After the watery blood came out of Mom's nose I witnessed Mom's breathing changed to one of the body struggling to inhale, but not succeeding. She went through the motions of inhalation only to get a little air, but it was mostly exhalation. Mom's whole body then tried to lift up as if she was making one last desperate attempt to inhale, but was unable to, and then a big last blowing-out of air occurred. The lungs had collapsed. Lastly, a few small motions emerged as if the unconscious breathing was still trying to continue, but failed. At this moment, I was holding the front part of Mom's feet with my thumb pressing on the bottom of the feet at Kidney-1 area. I was holding her the whole time throughout the final breath. Seems the Holy Spirit was sending Qi through the Kidney-1 point. I was doing this somehow unconsciously, but according to Joy, it was the right thing to have done. And then a huge wave of sadness flooded over me and I cried. I cried a lot. This wave seemed like it was Mom's soul leaving her body."

The work that Terry and I provided for Julie's natural conscious dying taught me that distance supervision of natural conscious dying at home is possible. Being surrounded with loved ones is a valuable treasure to the dying person. Julie's case has cleared my doubts and wonders about the importance of dying naturally and consciously. It validates the possibility of dying comfortably with minimum drug intake to none, and proceeding in the most natural way. Applying natural healing remedies can help keep chemical drug usage to a minimum, possibly even to zero, for these terminally ill people. The positive effect is to gain as much consciousness as possible so they can fully experience their dying process. This is so important to each and every soul.

Later on, I asked Terry, "What did you think about using small doses of morphine to help mom's breathing? Do you think it is beneficial?" Terry replied, "I didn't see the benefit of using morphine at all for conscious dying. With natural remedies and proper care, people can have peacefully transition without much suffering. Mom received two small doses of morphine because my dad panicked and didn't know how to help her. Taking care of a dying loved one is tiring and emotional. However, if people love their parents and want the best for them, conscious dying is the most beautiful choice for your loved ones. If I can do it, anybody can do it. Your professional supervision is necessary to guide the process, as well as to know what to expect." As Terry said, "Without your guidance and support, this conscious dying wouldn't have happened with my mom. I deeply appreciate your help and your time."

From this in-home-conscious-dying case, we can understand the extent of work required of doctors and hospitals to take care of each patient's dying process. In contrast, for each individual family, the death of their loved one is precious, beyond words. This is especially true for families who have spiritual beliefs and would like to treasure the moment of soul transformation, such as Julie's natural conscious dying. Without that insight, the death process could lead a bigger loss and trauma to the surviving loved ones. In old times, people living in tight communities were taken care of naturally by each other, family, friends, neighbors, and villagers. Today, given all the demands of modern life, it would be an overwhelming task for any particular family to handle the dying process alone. It is best this is when professionals as well as community need to come together to help this human evolutionary process. I strongly suggest that TCM methods of care are invaluable at this time. Equally, TCM would be a tremendous adjunct to the hospice palliative care model.

CHAPTER 10

"YOUR HELP PUSHED HER OUT OF THE MUD"

I will at this point describe my dream I had related to the work we did for Julie, which for me was profound and life changing. This dream inspired and deeply informed my passion to help people die in a natural conscious way.

The most important and clearest message gleaned from my dream concerned work we did for Julie, centered on this sentence: "YOUR HELP PUSHED HER OUT OF THE MUD!" This was the very first time I had heard this kind of spiritual expression. It indicated to me the importance of supporting a dying person in retaining consciousness. Besides this core message, there were more spiritual messages displayed inside my dream. Here is the recollection of my dream:

I went up to a place that appeared to be some kind of a heavenly station to ask for help. I rushed into a large room, it might have been a temple, or even a classroom. I indicated to the people there that I had come to ask for help for Julie. I saw a woman and two other people. They told me they were preparing something for her. When they pointed to a white seated Buddha statue, I hesitated, feeling it was not the right statue. My eyes moved away from it. One of the women brought another one out, quickly saying, "This one is for her." It was a white marble seated Buddhist statue similar to the first one, but the head and hair-style were different. It had a female quality. It represented a Quan Yin Buddhist statue in my mind. In addition, there was a golden sash placed on her left shoulder which crossed over and down to her right waist. She continued, "We will also light this one for her." She was holding a sparkler stick, like the fourth of July sparkler. The Quan Yin statue was very beautiful, and pure white. I was looking at it, feeling very content and satisfied.

Then, I walked away down a long balcony, visiting other rooms. When I returned to the original room I saw the statue was still there, it had not yet been sent out. I was a little anxious and said, "Why hasn't it been sent yet?" They said, "It is almost ready." Then, I saw a monk, young, fit and very handsome, preparing things. He was putting on a big bright golden-colored robe on himself. I asked why the sparkler stick was still not lit? Why wait? He said, "It will be ready in a minute." The Quan Yin statue was then put on a swing and the stick was lit. It sparkled and shone brightly on the white statue, catching the golden-colored sash over her shoulder. The monk jumped on the swing. There were people on the roof holding the rope. I could not see them clearly. They seemed to loosen the rope of the swing and drop him down very quickly. I looked down, seeing clouds moving, but could not see the ground. However, hearing cheers from below, it seemed there was a big gathering down there. He flew in the air and happily swung up and down a few times, and then swung back to the room with a big happy smile. I heard voices. People down there were asking me who he was. I shouted out in a loud voice, "He is a monk!"

After that, I saw myself land on the ground. There were many people gathered there, cheering with happiness and joy. They looked as if they were busy working on saving and pulling newly arrived people out of something like wells, waiting for their family members to arrive. To the left side there was a big ocean and there were people walking near the beach. Many people were walking in front of me.

At this moment, a voice or a message said to me, "Your help pushed her out of the mud." It was a very strong message. Then further messages came to me, saying it was because she was pushed out of the "mud", so that they could find her. Someone said I should be rewarded because the part of the work I, or better said we, had done was the initial and most critical stage of this project of "saving a person's soul", or could be understood as liberating a soul from Earth. It turned out that what we had done was worth 25% of the entire process of liberating a soul. I received no answer to the question of who would affect the other 75%. Likely, a monk sending a Buddha statue somewhere counted as a part of the 75% process. This big crowd seemed as if they were still working on saving her life or that of many other persons. This message indicated to me, although there were only a few steps in liberating a soul, it definitely involved team work.

I kept hearing the joyful celebration. All of these people were involved in helping to save lives or liberate souls from Earth.

Then I moved to a nearby garden, where the ground was made of concrete. There was a ditch there filled with water, and tall green plants with wide long leaves that looked like corn plants. There were no people around there. The concrete floor was covered with clear and clean water. There were many frogs, big green ones, stationed next to each other. They looked like they formed the edges of the ditch. I looked at them closely, some were jumping, but most were sitting next to each other, quite still… Then I woke up with the chanting in my mind…

What have I learned and interpreted from my dream? What do all these spiritual messages mean? I'm not certain even today. Perhaps it is the need to listen to our intuition and allow that faculty to give us greater insights into our life. From one perspective it might seem that my dream was a response of my unconscious to the course of Julie's dying and my concerns.

Readers might argue that I was emotionally and psychically touched by Julie's dying process and the images in my dream were simply a response to this. Perhaps. But this is certain: my dream itself gave me greater spiritual guidance by inspiring me to respond from a deeper and more compassionate level to the healing work of natural conscious dying.

My spiritual belief follows Chinese traditions, Buddhism and Taoism, however, my knowledge about the spiritual world is limited. After researching the symbols from my dream from various religious contexts, I am able to absorb further important spiritual information. Here, I am going to analyze certain aspects of my dream to share the deeper spiritual messages or insights.

My strongest desire is to better understand the symbolic meaning of mud in spiritual terms. This message of "your help pushed her out of the mud" was such a powerful insight that stuck in my mind and boosted my urge to eagerly research the meanings of "mud" in different religions. I believe, this is the key word that lead me to understand the significance of helping people dying consciously.

The following are mud as metaphors in different religious contexts.

The Meaning of "Mud" in Theravada Buddhism

After the dream, the word "mud" kept spinning in my head. I firstly contacted a college friend who has been deeply practicing Buddhism for a long time. I expected he would give me some information about the meaning of mud in Buddhism. My friend quickly responded to my request. In the teachings of Theravada Buddhism mud refers to the state of hell. There are eighteen layers of hell, called Ni Li. "Ni 泥" means mud, "Li 黎" ditch. Ni Li thus can be direct translated as "mud ditch".

Two days later, I went to do volunteer work as a Chinese medicine doctor at the City of Ten Thousand Buddhas in Ukiah, California. What a coincidence in timing! For me, it was a great retreat after this emotionally exhausting work. This event was arranged two weeks before Julie's death. Having a deep desire to learn more about the spiritual meaning of mud in Buddhism, I shared the story of Julie's conscious dying and my dream to the head nun of the medical center. She explained to me that "mud" indicates a place blocking people's spiritual growth, thus it is called hell.

The term Ni Li (泥黎), was actually translated from Sanskrit in the second century C.E.. This person's Chinese name was An Shi Gao, who was thought to be Parthamasiris of Armenia. He came to China during the period of 147-167at the time of the East Han Dynasty. An Shi Gao was the first person to translate many Buddhist Dharma books from Sanskrit to Chinese. Among them, one book is called *Buddha talking about 18 layers of NiLi (Hells)*. Ni Li is translated as "HELL", a place described as having no redeeming qualities, no happiness or joy.

One day I listened to a Chinese Buddhist song on YouTube. The song sounded like a psalm, praising Manjushri, the Bodhisattva of wisdom. Inside this long praying to Manjushri, there is a sentence which reads:

"…Due to falling in this pleasure sea of mud
we cannot move. Dear Manjushri Bodhisattva with your love
and compassion, please save us out of this mud…"[4]

In this chant, mud directly means something that

blocks a person's movement.

The Meaning of "Mud" in Christianity

One Sunday, I went with my family to a local Christian church. There was a large framed painting of a religious scene that caught my attention. I was excited to see it. I told myself I had found the answer to my dream! Only I alone could understand how much this painting meant to me.

The painting is called: *POLIPTICO DEL JUICIO FINAL* in Spanish. It is translated as *Polytical of The Final Judgment*. The artist is Roger van der Weyden (1399 or 1400—18 June 1464), a famous painter from the Netherlands. The painting shows many naked humans in different positions inside the mud, some raising an arm to reach the saints who were majestically sitting in Heaven. Saint Peter, sitting in the middle, held a scale in his hands with a naked man on it. It represents the act of judgment by those heavenly saints. People who were saved were walking toward a church-like building. Those people who could not be saved were left in the mud.

Mud is a thick sticky unclear substance which can trap things inside it. Free movement is not possible in mud. Thus, one of the spiritual metaphors of mud refers to being stuck. Mud is the main solid surface substance of earth. What is buried inside mud cannot easily escape. The second metaphor of mud most likely refers to the earth bound dimension like the painting of *The Final Judgement*. Thus, those souls are not able to return to the Heavenly realm are left stuck in the mud.

Apparently, in Buddhist dharma teachings "mud" refers to 'hell', a place which traps people inside its confines and blocks their conscious growth and soul ascension. The 'pleasure sea of mud' is a layer of hell that attracts people seeking pleasure, and makes them turn away from spiritual growth and soul ascension. "Soul ascension" apparently refers to those souls who have escaped from the earth bound realm and have returned to the heavenly dimension.

The Meaning of "Mud" in Taoism

In Taoist tradition, there is a place in the human brain called "mud pill palace (泥丸宫)". Apparently, there is a "mud pill" inside it. Taoist spirituality argues a human being's main soul, which is called "Yuan Shen 元神," is most likely this "mud pill (泥丸)". In modern scientific terms, this "mud pill palace" likely corresponds to the place where the pineal gland or third-eye resides. When one dies in a conscious way, this "mud pill palace" may open and releases the mud pill, "Yuan Shen" out into the cosmic space. A Chinese expression is: "soul bursting out of orifices" (Ling Hun Chu Qiao 灵魂 出窍). The orifices are the energy openings that connect the body to the outer space. In other words, the third eye may be opened and released into the cosmic, spiritual world.

If a person dies without consciousness that likely indicates this "mud pill palace" is closed. Mud pill "Yuan Shen" could not come out from the top of head, but is left inside the body or exits from another place. Thus, the soul is not able to free itself from the confines of the earth. In this way it is akin to being buried inside the "mud". If a person is dying with awareness, it could be argued that that very consciousness will be 'captured' by the spiritual world. Angels or higher beings would then come to help this person's soul transition and liberation.

The Critical Step in Dying

The dream continued telling me how important this conscious awakening process itself is. It is the very first critical step in saving and liberating the soul, even though it consumes only about 25% of the entire process. However, if this 25% were absent, souls would not be identified, and would simply remain in the "mud". It makes me wonder how many souls are left in the "mud" due to high doses of chemical drugs like morphine? Certainly, it is hard to count. If our medical system were to encourage this process of 25% of soul transitioning, it would definitely bring very different outcomes to our societies.

Spirit Guide

Now we return to the question of who was this handsome monk? What did sending the statue and sparkling light mean? Why was I so anxious for them to hurry up?

The monk in my dream was relaxed and very happy. It seemed that sending the Buddha statue was his duty: he was not in a rush, but was measured and controlled. He knew what needed to happen. Likely knowing Julie would not live much longer, I was anxious that the process should move ahead.

Was this monk a spirit guide? Inside my dream, when people from way down below asked me who he was as he flew down on the swing with a Buddha statue and a sparkling light. Then I shouted loudly, "He is a monk!" What does sending a statue mean here? I am not quite sure. The monk represented a Buddhist spiritual tradition. Many traditions believe when one is dying, angels, spirit guides, or higher spiritual beings come to greet or pick one up and guide one where one belongs.

Reader may argue that my mind tried to get clarity about Julie's dying. There were male and female Buddha statues brought to me, most likely the male statue was prepared for a male dying person, and the Quan Yin statue was for a female dying person. These people in my dream quickly realized I came asking for help for a female. They also provided one sparkling stick which I am not certain its metaphor. I thought it might have lit Julie's life for one more day. In fact, Julie did wake up in the morning and died the following morning.

In my dream, the "people" in the big crowd were in the spiritual world. I felt like these people were already transitioned family members, waiting to save or greet their newly deceased family members. Many of them were actively engaged in helping and cherishing these new arrivals. These dying people seemed like beings who came off a "train" or being pulled out of wells with family members waiting for them to arrive. This reminds me of the phenomenon which happened to Jay at the very end. He burst out in a big smile, saying three times, "grandma, my family, …".

The dying process is the transitioning from the physical body to the cosmic conscious soul life.

This dying process is undoubtedly dependent on team work, involving not only those who are close family members and friends on Earth, but also those from the spirit world.

Eternal life is hard to understand within one human life time. Spiritual wisdom and knowledge are known to be passed on through spiritual lineages. Whether one believes it or not, our consciousness is connected through all dimensions. Perhaps one day we may realize spirits are communicating with us all the time. The truth is we do not know how to listen to our own souls, nor do we know how to listen to spirits. Dying is a natural part of life. Should we not seek a natural conscious way of dying as a significant part of our spiritual practice on Earth? Yes, we should.

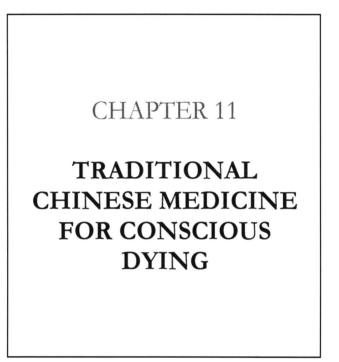

CHAPTER 11

TRADITIONAL CHINESE MEDICINE FOR CONSCIOUS DYING

As we approach the end of this book, there is one final point I would like to make: How do the tools of TCM, specifically acupuncture and moxibustion, work to help the natural dying process? It is well established that acupuncture can treat a wide variety of pain-related conditions and the conditions like anxiety, depression, fatigue, constipation, flu, common cold, allergies, and so on. One of the common experiences for all of those who experience acupuncture and moxibustion is a feeling of being energized. Feeling energized is actually a healthy state human should naturally experience. All physiological, emotional and spiritual activities require energy, and crucially even to the dying process.

Traditional Chinese Medicine (TCM) has been around for 3,000 years. Acupuncture and moxibustion are the two main methods of physical treatment. Often a technique called Hui Yang Jiu Zhen (回阳九针), which means "Nine Needles Revive Yang Qi" (Yang symbolizes vitality energy), is used to revive the one who is unconscious or lifeless. When combined with moxibustion treatment, it helps to increase the body's Yang Qi and promote blood flow. Used together, it helps to revive consciousness and life. There are a few acu-points on the body that have the same function.

Many lives can be quickly saved with this technique. In Jay's case, his consciousness was present, alive, and communicated with us to the very end. This situation is a definite validation of this technique in working with a dying person.

There are many ways people can help their loved one going through dying process naturally. Using acupuncture and moxibustion for people on their death bed is a new idea in the modern world. This is not surprising because TCM is still new to western culture. If people who want to help their loved ones with TCM, he/she can be trained from an experienced TCM practitioner or under their supervision. Natural conscious dying (NCD) training will be available at Heavenly Joy Institute.

Nowadays, due to a medical crisis, people are finding themselves in hospitals at the end of their life. As soon as conventional medicine has nothing more to offer, hospice is often brought in for palliative care using convenient protocols of chemical drug applications and other comfort care. The work of the hospice movement is a tremendous innovation, with its goal of helping people become aware of a real and different way of spending their last days. However, a completely NDC protocol isn't available yet. A NDC protocol will provide a really great service to humanity, especially to those who value their spiritual growth.

Let us now focus on the Yin and Yang aspects for aged people.

In TCM, all illness is the result of imbalance or deficiency in Yin or Yang aspects inside the body. The vitality of any life depends on the balance and the amount of Yin and Yang. An easier way to explain how Yin and Yang actually work in a human body is by looking at the mechanical principles rather than biochemical reactions. When people move into their 80s and 90s, their physical bodies have grown depleted in Qi and blood. Often one hears people saying, "I'm getting dried up", referring to growing old. This is actually true. It refers to the Yin aspect of the body such as body fluids, water and blood which are becoming depleted. At the same time, we often see older people feeling cold, moving slowly, eating less, and getting sick easily. This is due to the Yang aspect of the body where the life fire, the Qi (energy), and the transformation abilities are low. Naturally, human aging is the process of exhausting Yang (life fire), Qi (energy), blood, and bodily fluids. Again, this can be present in the elderly population as the loss of strength, mobility, skin elasticity, hair color, mental functioning, and etc. In fact, if Yang, Qi, blood or bodily fluids, are exhausted early in life, death can arrive well ahead of time. In TCM, we recognize that chronic illness usually indicates one or several organs as being weak or depleted. In addition, we believe that depletion of the Yin-Yang aspects of the body has a direct adverse impact on cognition, learning abilities, and emotional well-being. Thus, TCM theory indicates that mind, spirit, and emotions are all affected by physical well-being.

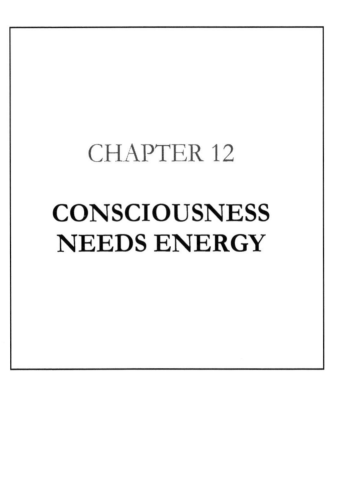

CHAPTER 12

CONSCIOUSNESS NEEDS ENERGY

In TCM theory, mind, spirit, and emotional activities are called Shen, the same term used for consciousness. Shen is supported by having the proper amount of Qi, blood, and bodily fluids. To explain how these aspects work together in the human body, I will use the simple analogy of heating a kettle. A kettle (body) with a steam whistle (brain) is filled up with water (Yin), and then put on the top of a stove with fire (Yang). When the stove's fire is turned on and strong enough, the water inside the kettle boils to produce steam. The steam is Qi, Qi, thus blows the whistle (brain), and a loud sound (consciousness, mind, and emotional activities) is generated. This awakens consciousness to communicate many dimensions including to spiritual realm. The loud sound (consciousness) can be heard and felt from far away.

How does this relate to the dying process?

While dying consciously, it is very important for the soul to make connections with the body through this consciousness, helping the dying transition to complete itself. However, if the fire on the stove is too low, only a small stream of vapor will be produced. If there is no water in the kettle, there will be no steam at all. If the dying person does not have enough of the Yang Qi (the vibrant fire), consciousness cannot be activated. The stronger the Qi, the more awake and active the expression of consciousness. The Qi and consciousness therefore work together, enlivening each other. From the example of the kettle we can extrapolate and draw a conclusion that when the Qi and blood have been exhausted completely, a person's Shen (consciousness) will be completely still. This may explain why a dying one is most often unconscious or in a coma.

You may have been pondering how acupuncture and moxibustion play a role in the process of conscious-dying. As you can now understand, consciousness needs energy (Qi) to support it. Acupuncture and moxibustion provide Yang Qi to the body through a few specific acupuncture points. They support Qi and the blood flow to help the body fulfil the essential life processes. If the human body is abundant with Qi and blood, life thrives. However, if one's condition has moved into the irreversible dying process, then Yang Qi can help to revive one's consciousness, thus allowing the body to complete the dying process.

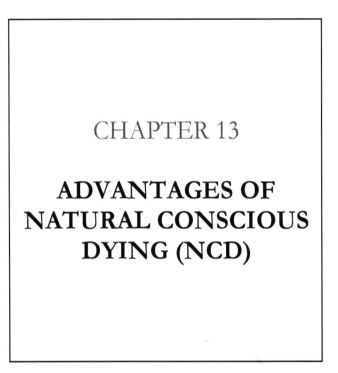

CHAPTER 13

ADVANTAGES OF NATURAL CONSCIOUS DYING (NCD)

There is a healthy way of living and there is a healthy way of dying. The wisdom of living, as TCM teaches us, is to prevent disease from happening. If people follow this living principle to the end of life, they might even be able to predict the date of their end of life transition. They can pass away peacefully while resting. This is one of the great values of natural conscious dying. It is called good death in many old traditions. Living up to a given age and dying without illness is the true longevity and real happiness of life. Everyone should strive for this healthy cycle of life on Earth.

During all these years, I kept searching for the perfect answers to the question of why conscious dying is important. A trip with my daughter to Singapore in 2016 brought me some insightful understandings. My good friend Gigi Ho took me to visit a 78-year-old Buddhist monk who deeply practices early Theravada Buddhist dharma. His daily work provides spiritual guidance to elderly people, people who are on their dying beds or have extreme trauma injuries.

The following is my understanding derived from his teaching. First, our mind, thought or consciousness helps us to make choices about the life we are living as well as the life after death. Conscious awareness is like a compass helping us choose where to go. Conscious dying helps us mentally, spiritually, and physically prepare for a natural transition which avoids struggling with all unknown situations. Second, emotional energies of the last moment will leave a blueprint on our souls.

The emotions or memories will transform into energies that remain in our souls when they exit the body. Our personalities may not be given by our parents but rather likely by our soul's energies when incarnation occurs. The last moment of conscious energy will directly affect the soul's journey.

There are different ways of dying, ranging from an abrupt and violent death to a natural process of peaceful aging and dying. Unnatural death often refers to unpredicted events such as a violent fight, car or airplane crash, animal attack, or other accidents. Most people, in cases like these, do die instantly and also consciously. This type of death, however, cannot be considered a good death. These last moments of the energies of emotions and thoughts will leave blueprints on the consciousness of the soul. This type of death is not what we have been talking about because it is unpredictable.

In this book, we are talking about those people who are on their death beds due to causes such as medical conditions, or simply due to their aging. How can we prepare or help these people die in a natural peaceful way rather than applying many pharmaceutical drugs unnecessarily? This is the purpose of this book. There are methods that can be taken and put into effect to release physical discomfort while increasing consciousness and physical strength with TCM remedies. All of this information will be soon available in courses and a manual of Natural Conscious Dying (NCD) through Heavenly Joy Institute.

Conscious Awareness Allows Self-Refection

The beauty of conscious dying in a natural way allows the dying process itself to unfold with its own natural rhythm. During this process people often undertake self-reflection and are able to bring love and clarity to their souls. At the same time this process boosts the soul's energy for the next steps.

Among many, one of the most important aspects we can offer to help those who are dying is to clear their emotional baggage. When a person's mind and thoughts are so attached to their emotions or material things, their daily actions are often emotionally driven. In this way, they tend to be in total control and they don't let things go. These heavy emotions can influence their consciousness as well as their physical wellbeing.

If a dying person's conscious mind is clear, happy, tranquil, and peaceful, their soul will be exhibiting and carrying this joyful, tranquil, and peaceful energy. Their soul can exit easily and retain this energy that is of the nature of God, Buddha, the cosmic consciousness, or the TAO. If a dying person's conscious mind is unclear, sad, angry, worried, frightened, harboring resentment, greed, hate, or strong attachment to the family or a particular person, this soul will likely be driven by these energies. Ways to release these energies and continue these attachments via reincarnation will surely be found. Clearing some of these energies before dying is essential for one's soul ascension and growth.

Conscious dying can happen at different levels of consciousness. For example, GG in case 3, and Jay in case 4, as well as Julie in case 5, were experiencing noticeably different circumstances so they transitioned in different ways. You may have observed or noticed other people dying in various ways. When people come to the end of their life, if they are conscious, there is a natural urge to release past unresolved issues before death. Their human egos start to reduce and yearn to be cleansed, with a desire for forgiving and being forgiven. Making time to have conversations with the dying and helping them resolve their issues can bring great comfort to them.

Spiritual practice can help people shed emotional attachments and allow cosmic consciousness to flow inside, so they can recognize the nature of the Buddha, God, or TAO. Cultivating such peaceful tranquility and joy--the true nature of this cosmic consciousness--can only be done when one is conscious and awake. Engaging in spiritual practice as early as possible surely benefits conscious dying at the end.

Soul Up-Loading in Natural Rhythm

In Taoist and TCM teachings, the practice of aligning human consciousness with cosmic consciousness is commonly called Heaven-Human unity. Through this practice, human consciousness can remain clear, healthy and intact in the physical body to the end. Life is able to run on its own rhythm and evolve naturally in perfect harmony with universal laws. When dying happens, it is like a process similar to giving birth to a child, and should not be hurried. Giving enough time to allow souls to "up-load" is a healthy process for the life of the soul. Is not the idea of using "soul shed" to carry this soul "up-loading" process a great honor to the dead?

Traditional Chinese Medicine like many other ancient healing arts offers natural healing and energy to the human body. It helps to release physical discomfort, helps awaken consciousness (Shen Shi 神识), and thus it can support human natural conscious dying. For all those who consciously die with the support of TCM, it will give them an increased chance of completing these human tendencies before death. They will experience their transition with greater clarity and peace.

Being a Ritual Event

NCD adds the ritual aspects to the dying event. As an old Chinese saying, "By observing death, one knows how life works." A great experience is the witnessing of the dying event itself. It opens people up to the existence of the spiritual world and allows people to receive the lessons from other people's life.

Jay's conscious dying highlights some beautiful and blissful moments. We might never have known them had we not witnessed the dying ourselves. It is a precious moment to witness the instance when the spirit is about to leave the body. When the soul starts leaving the body it becomes aware of heaven or divine nature. By being conscious while dying, the dying person may be able to relate what they are experiencing to their family and friends around them. These experiences are tremendously profound and fulfilling. They can impact people in a very beneficial way. It can truly be a dying person's last gift to their loved ones.

To conclude, dying is a part of life one should not treat lightly. Being conscious while dying helps the soul choose a far more purposeful direction and journey. It encourages the soul to understand its true nature and how it relates to life. It helps the dying return to the light of the soul, even indicating in which direction to go and how to reincarnate. It may also increase the understanding of reincarnation for whomever is witnessing the dying event. As is the belief in Chinese tradition and many other older traditions, a good ending makes for a good beginning in the next life!

GLOSSARY

Acu-points: Refers to acupuncture points. There are 365 major energy points around the entire body according to TCM. They form energy channels and meridians that connect internal and external aspects of the body.

Acupuncture: An ancient healing art from TCM uses a solid needle to puncture through dermal (skin) layer to connect channels and meridians. This technique helps the human body unblock any stagnations or various blockages and promote blood and energy flow in channels. An easy way to understand how acupuncture works is to think about the mechanism of a plumbing system. When blockage happens, a problem can be created throughout the whole system. Unblocking the flow can resolve the problems.

Bardo: Life after death in an intermediate state between death and reincarnation.

Chakra: The Sanskrit term for energy centers inside the human body.

DAOM: Doctoral degree in Acupuncture and Oriental Medicine (DAOM).

Di Hun 地魂 (Earth Hun): Closely translates as subtle soul. "Di Hun" can return back to the heavenly realm through Tian Hun. Although this phenomenon remains a mystery, it might be understood in the future through Quantum Physics or String Theory.

Five fortunes: In one of the very oldest Chinese historical books, Shang Shu（尚书）, the sequence of the five fortunes, is represented as the following:

1) Shou 寿：Health and longevity, having abilities to live and fully develop a life span;

2) Fu 富: Abundance, having abilities to have a place to live and food to eat;

3) Kang Ning 康宁：Peaceful and tranquil, the ability to be happy and content and enjoy what is provided;

4) You Hao De 攸好德: Enjoy good nature and seeking to help others;

5) Kao Zhong Ming 考終命: Having abilities to predict the due date of life's ending, life ends peacefully without any unpredicted trauma and diseases.

https://zh.wikipedia.org/wiki/%E4%BA%94%E7%A6%8F

Hui Guang Fan Zhao (回光返照): Here in this book, it is translated as "Returned light shining back". It has been translated by others in the modern term as "the last radiance of the setting sun" or "momentary recovery of consciousness just before death".

Hui Yang Jiu Zhen (回阳九针): "Nine Needles Revive Yang Qi", an acupuncture technique documented in this Chinese book, 《针灸聚英》 (Zhen Jiu Ju Ying), "*Encyclopedia of Acupuncture and Moxibustion*", vol. 4-2, is a TCM technique to revive Yang Qi, consciousness, and save lives. There are nine specific acupuncture points are used to serve this purpose. They are Du15 哑门, Ht 8 劳宫, Sp6 三阴交，K1 涌泉，K3 太溪，R12 中脘，GB30 环跳，St36 足三里，Li4 合谷. These points are listed in a form of a rhyme: The Rhyme of Nine Needles Revive Yang Qi, or Chinese rhyme: "回阳九针歌" (Hui Yang Jiu Zhen Ge) is as the following:

歌诀为：哑门劳宫三阴交，涌泉太溪中脘接，环跳三里合谷并，此是回阳九针穴。

Hun 魂: Represents the energetic bodies associated with Shen that can come in and out of the human body, defined as the ethereal Soul. It is the Yang aspect of the soul which leaves the body after death (ShuoWenJieZi) and returns to the heaven realm.

Karma: Generally speaking, it is every action of each individual which causes either positive or negative effects in their future. Traditionally, every good and bad deed will be documented in the soul's memory.

Ling Peng (灵棚): A direct translation is "Soul Shed", it is a temporary tent-like structure for people who have just died. It is a Chinese tradition to allow dead ones to stay here for three to seven days to complete the dying process, and also for people to have a memorial moment with the dead ones.

Ling Hun Chu Qiao (灵魂出窍): A direct translation is "soul bursting out of orifices". If a person who is alive experiences this, it is like an out-of-body experience. It is a common expression in Chinese culture for one's spirit-soul to leave the physical body. It is often observed in dying people seen in spiritual practice.

Ming Hun 命魂 (Life soul or Life Hun): Controls the length of a person's life, physical flexibility and all physical movements and abilities.

Moxa: Abbreviation of moxibustion, a type of healing using Wormwood for burning to create heat which penetrates to the body through acupuncture points. It brings Yang energy to the body to increase vitality.

Moxa box: A wooden box that holds moxa herbs to burn, and prevent the ashes away from falling onto the skin by providing a safe distance from the patient.

Ni Li (泥黎): It was translated from Sanskrit as 'Hell'. Hells in Sanskrit, are jails under the earth. There are big or small jails, a place having nothing, with no happiness or joy. This earliest translation likely comes from this book called, *Buddhist talking about Eighteen Hells (Ni Li)*《佛说十八泥黎经》. It is one of the earliest translated books by An Shi Gao (安世高), who is believed to be Parthamasiris of Armenia in the research by Cheng Jun Feng in 1930s. An Shi Gao stayed in China from 147 to 167 C. E. at East Han Dynasty. After he came in China, China started to have Buddhist dharma teachings and philosophy.

Later, a monk named Pu Run in Song Dynasty, lived in Gu Su Jing De Temple, collected this term, among many others, Ni Li as "hell" in this book, <*Translation of Terminology, vol. 7, No.26, Chapter on Discussion of Hells*) 《翻译名义集卷》第七， 地狱篇第二十六。宋姑苏景德寺普润大师法云编。

Natural Conscious Dying (NCD): Is a natural dying process without using chemical drugs. Acupuncture and natural thermal devices such as moxa box or rice heating pads may be applied to the acupressure points to help release physical discomforts.

Po 魄: Refers to the spirits that attach to the physical body and form the Yin aspect of soul as corporeal soul. After people die, Po remains with the corpse of the deceased and return to earth (ShuoWenJieZi).

(http://www.zdic.net/z/28/xs/9B42.htm)

Shen 神: Represents the mystical cosmic energy that alchemizes and connects everything in the universe. A similar term can be interpreted and understood as the cosmic consciousness of the universe (ShuoWenJieZi).

Soul Shed: A temporary tent-like structure built outside of the home for the dying to continue their transition, often decorated in white, called Ling Peng (See Ling Peng).

Taoism: The very root of spiritual belief and traditional Chinese culture. It states that all beings are interconnected as part of the cosmic universal law. Human life follows the nature of heaven and earth, living harmoniously with all beings.

TCM: Abbreviation of Traditional Chinese Medicine.

Tian Hun 天魂 (Heaven Hun): Close translates as astral soul which enters and leaves the body. In Taoist belief, when a person is dying the astral soul is the first soul to leave the body.

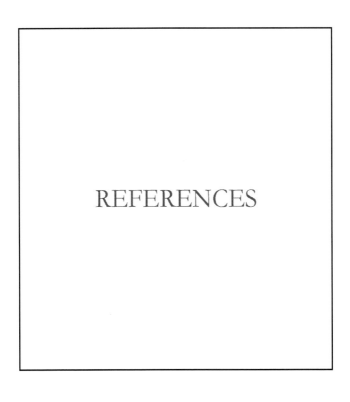

REFERENCES

Evans-Wentz, W. Y. (2000): *The Tibetan Book of The Dead*. Oxford University Press.

Huang Di Nei Jing is a classic book of Traditional Chinese Medicine from 200-300 B.C.E.

Kettley, Sebastian (2018): Life After Death: What happens when you die? What happens after death?

Aug.1, 2018, https://www.express.co.uk/news/science/997375/Life-after-death-what-happens-when-you-die-afterlife-proof-science-news

Martin, Sean (2018) Life after death? Woman 'meets angel' in shock glimpse of the afterlife

May 9, 2018, https://www.express.co.uk/news/weird/957103/life-after-death-what-happens-when-you-die-proof-of-heaven-god-angel

Osis, Karlis and Haraldsson, Erlendur (1972): *At the Hour of Death*: A New Look at *Evidence for Life After Death*. White Crow Books. First edition.

Shang Shu (尚书) (Zhou dynasty): One of the

Five Classics of Ancient Chinese literature. Zhou （周） China, Language in Old Chinese, Subject: Compilation of rhetorical prose. Chapter 《洪範》 means "big laws".

ShuoWenJieZi (说文解字): The oldest dictionary explaining Chinese written language, it contains 9353 words. Appeared in the Eastern Han dynasty around 100-122 A.D.

Weyden, Roger van der: The Final judgment. Visita virtual: POLIPTICO DEL JUICIO FINAL, espiritualidad amenazante en un hospital, (Tournai, 1400-Bruselas, 1464).

http://domuspucelae.blogspot.com/2013/01/visitavirtual-poliptico-del-juicio.html

Wu, Tianyun (2014): Conscious Dying by TCM, clinical cases. Preventive Medicine: Yang Sheng and Traditional Chinese Medicine 10-Types of Physical Constitution, Doctoral Dissertation of University of East-West Medicine, Sunnyvale, California.

Wu, Tianyun (2018): (unpublished), *Manual of Natural Conscious Dying*, to learn more about NCD, please visit: www.heavenlyjoyinstitute.org.

Songs from YouTube:

1. *Amazing Grace sung by Leann Rimes*

https://www.youtube.com/watch?v=iT88jBAoVIM

2. *How Great Thou Art*

https://www.youtube.com/watch?v=0HJYZj8PqEY

3. *Shine, Jesus, Shine*

https://www.youtube.com/watch?v=7OIwSQmyCg4

4. Praising Manjushri, the Bodhisattva of wisdom,
https://www.youtube.com/Patch?v=NHwuxeum8sE

ABOUT THE AUTHOR

Dr. Joy Tianyun Wu grew from a successful and modern life scientist in molecular biology to an educator and primary healthcare provider of Traditional Chinese Medicine and Acupuncture. Joy is inspired by the Taoist philosophy of Heaven-Human Unity: Things are done to benefit all and harm none. She is passionate about bringing to the world Taoist wisdom of disease prevention and harmonious living. Natural Conscious Dying is one of many innovative programs in her non-profit organization, Heavenly Joy Institute.

On the side of practice of TCM, Dr. Wu is developing on-line certification programs for current medical practitioners and those interested in working with Natural Conscious Dying. Services and spiritual counseling are available for individuals. Please visit www.heavenlyjoyinstitute.org to learn or support these programs.